# Why Do De Novo Banks Choose a National Charter?

**Gary W. Whalen**

*Office of the Comptroller of the Currency*

**OCC Economics Working Paper 2010-2**

May 2010

Keywords: Dual banking system; charter choice; de novo bank.
JEL classifications: G21, G28, L51.

Gary W. Whalen is a Senior Economic Advisor in the Policy Analysis Division of the Office of the Comptroller of the Currency, 250 E St., SW, Washington, DC 20219. Please address correspondence to the author (phone 202-874-4441; fax 202-874-5394; e-mail: gary.whalen@occ.treas.gov).

The views expressed in this paper are those of the author alone and do not necessarily reflect those of the Office of the Comptroller of the Currency or the U.S. Department of the Treasury. The author would like to thank David Nebhut and Lewis Gaul for their comments and Janet Fix and Lily Chin for editorial assistance. The author takes responsibility for any errors.

# Why Do De Novo Banks Choose a National Charter?

Gary W. Whalen

May 2010

**Abstract:** Examination of the charter choices made by the more than 1,600 new banks established from 1998 through 2008 reveals that since 2003 there has been a clear and persistent shift in preference away from national bank charters and in favor of state bank charters. This study seeks to understand the primary reasons for this change in chartering behavior.

Various econometric models are used to analyze annual local market entry by de novo—or newly chartered—banks in 929 urban banking markets during the 11-year period. This analysis suggests that higher supervisory costs may make de novo national bank entry more sensitive to local market competitive conditions than is the case for state banks. Indicators of competition found to be important determinants of de novo national bank entry include state intrastate branching restrictions, market concentration, and de novo branching by out-of-market banking organizations.

The evidence indicates that state-specific supervisory disadvantages decrease the likelihood and extent of de novo national bank entry. Greater numbers of mergers and acquisitions of locally headquartered national banks also have a positive effect on de novo national bank entry, possibly because they reflect the availability of senior management familiar with and to national bank supervisors.

## I. Introduction

From 1998 through 2008, industry consolidation reduced the number of commercial banks in the United States by more than 20 percent.[1] Meanwhile, bank charter changes from merger and nonmerger activity combined to increase the share of assets held by national banks by more than 10 percentage points, up from the mid-50 percent level that prevailed throughout the 1980s and 1990s.[2] Some argue that this increased asset share reflects a significant competitive advantage for national banks, particularly for large organizations, possibly related to preemption determinations made by their supervisor, the Office of the Comptroller of the Currency (OCC).

A total of 1,663 de novo banks began operations between 1998 and 2008.[3] The charter choices made by de novo bankers during this period reveal a markedly different pattern of supervisory preferences. Figure 1 clearly shows that since 2003 there has been a persistent, sizeable shift by new banks away from the national charter. Previous researchers have investigated the determinants of de novo entry, charter choice by *established banks* and, only tangentially, the effect of charter choice on bank failure. They did not investigate the factors influencing charter choice by *newly established* banks.

---

[1] The number of commercial banks declined by 2,106 (22.6 percent) through June 2008, from 9,309 in June 1997.

[2] National bank asset share was 56.3 percent in June 1997, compared with 69.4 percent in June 2008.

[3] In this study annual de novo bank entry for a given year is measured from June 30 of that year through July 1 of the previous year. This approach makes it easier to match the de novo bank entry data to other variables used in the analysis that are derived from the Federal Deposit Insurance Corporation's Summary of Deposit (SOD) data. The SOD data show bank offices and deposits at the local level on June 30 each year. So de novo bank entry for 1998 represents all new banks (except industrial loan companies) established from July 1, 1997 through June 30, 1998.

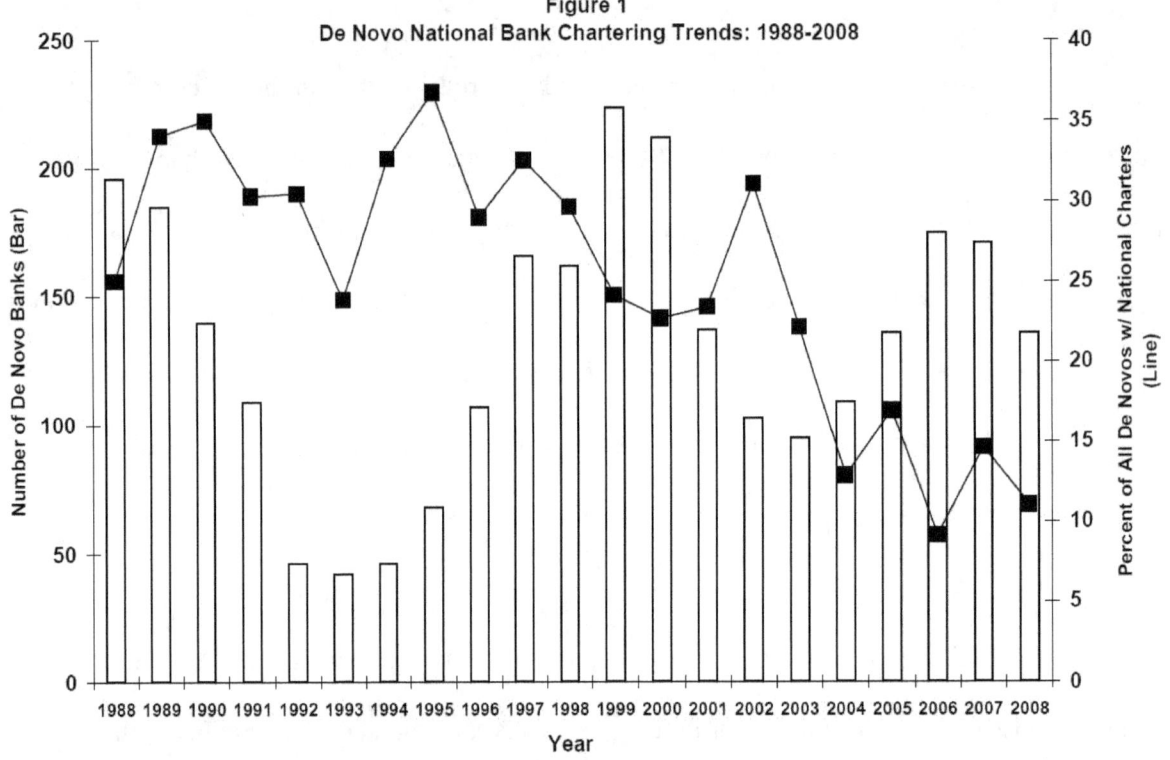

Figure 1
De Novo National Bank Chartering Trends: 1988-2008

Source: Author's calculations.

Research on this issue is important for several reasons. If the shift in favor of state bank charters is largely cost-driven, it highlights the potential importance of fee disparities and supervisory competition for constituents in charter choice.[4] Identifying the primary determinants of de novo charter choice also could provide insight into whether this trend is temporary or permanent. If the trend is permanent, it has the potential to influence the survival of the dual banking system.

The goal of this study is to identify determinants of the charter choices made by de novo banks from 1998 through 2008 to understand the reasons for the shift away from the national charter. Annual data for a sample of 929 urban banking markets are used to estimate several

---

[4] One potential drawback associated with the U.S. system (where banks choose their charter and primary regulator) is that competition for constituents by federal and state bank regulators could result in the progressive relaxation of supervisory constraints. This phenomenon has been labeled "competition in laxity."

different econometric models of local market entry by national and state-chartered de novo banks.[5]

The empirical evidence suggests that higher supervisory costs may make de novo entry by national banks more sensitive to local market competitive conditions than is the case for state banks. Indicators of competition found to be important determinants of de novo national bank entry include state intrastate branching restrictions, market concentration, and de novo branching by out-of-market banking organizations.

Evidence also indicates that state-specific supervisory disadvantages influence the likelihood and extent of de novo national bank entry. Greater numbers of mergers and acquisitions of locally headquartered national banks have a significant positive effect on de novo national bank entry, possibly because they increase the availability of senior management familiar with and to national bank supervisors.

The following section discusses the factors likely to influence the charter choices of de novo banks, particularly national banks. Section III examines de novo bank entry patterns. Section IV discusses the econometric techniques and estimated equations used in this study. Section V presents the estimation results. Section VI summarizes the results and conclusions.

---

[5] Urban geographic banking markets are approximated by metropolitan or micropolitan statistical areas (metro and micro areas), geographic entities defined by the Office of Management and Budget. Core-based statistical area is a collective term for both area types. A metro area contains an urban core of 50,000 or more population, while a micro area contains an urban core of at least 10,000 (but less than 50,000) population. Each metro and micro area includes one or more counties and the counties containing the core urban area as well as any adjacent counties that have a high degree of social and economic integration with the urban core. Counties that are not part of either metro or micro areas are assumed to approximate nonurban banking markets and are excluded from the analysis. The sample period starts in 1998 because the analysis requires lagged market structure variables, and the FDIC revised the Summary of Deposit data to a core-based statistical area basis only back to 1994.

## II. Influences on the Number of De Novo National Bank Entrants

The extent of de novo entry by national banks in any given period reflects the interplay of two sets of forces.

First, de novo entry by both national and state banks depends on local market condition variables that influence the expected profitability of de novo entrants generally. Because it takes time to organize a de novo bank and obtain approvals to open from state or federal authorities, current entry in any local market typically depends on lagged values of these explanatory variables.

A number of empirical studies (e.g., Adams and Amel 2007; Berger, Bonime, Goldberg, and White 2000; Keeton 2000; Seelig and Critchfield 2003) investigating the determinants of de novo bank local market entry have been published recently. The set of explanatory variables used in these studies is fairly consistent, although the precise definitions and lags vary. The right-hand side (RHS) variables used in the models include measures of market merger and acquisition activity, deposit shares of various size classes of banks, deposit shares of out-of-market organizations, market concentration, past market profitability, lagged entry, incumbent branching, state geographic restriction dummies, and various other market economic and demographic variables.

Second, the percentage of new banks choosing a national rather than a state charter depends on the magnitude of any charter-related advantages or disadvantages. Charter-related advantages and disadvantages may change over time and be amplified by market-specific forces that influence entry.[6] Most notably, more intense local market competition increases the burden of any charter-related disadvantage for de novo national banks.

---

[6] A bank's strategy can impact charter-related benefits and costs, but this issue is not explored in this study.

In the dual banking system, banks choose a national or state charter. The choice determines their supervisor(s) and influences permissible activities, applicable regulations, and supervisory costs. The OCC supervises national banks. State banks are supervised by a home state regulator and by the Federal Reserve Bank (Fed) or the Federal Deposit Insurance Corporation (FDIC).

Charter-related differences have generally narrowed over time, but several potentially important differences remain. Perhaps the most important and tangible difference is that national banks pay higher explicit supervisory costs than state banks.[7] A January 2002 OCC fee revision incorporating a minimum base amount increased the cost disadvantage for smaller national banks.[8]

Table 1 shows estimates of the explicit supervisory cost disadvantage that de novo national banks face in seven selected states.[9] The first column shows supervisory cost estimates for national banks in three asset categories—$25 million, $50 million, and $100 million.[10] The next seven columns show comparable estimates for similarly sized state banks in a small group of states with readily available fee schedules. The data in the column labeled State Average are the mean values of supervisory costs for the three size classes state banks in these seven states.

---

[7] A state bank pays a supervisory fee to its home state supervisor. Neither federal supervisor (the Fed or the FDIC) explicitly charges a state bank for supervision. Differences in supervisory costs for national and state banks are detailed in Blair and Kushmeider (2006, p.6). Supervisory competition might also result in significant differences in implicit costs across charter types. For example, "competition in laxity" could decrease implicit supervisory costs for certain charter types. Alternatively, Rosen (2003) hypothesizes that supervisors desire a "quiet life" and pressure problematic banks to change their charters. For anecdotal evidence on these cost differences, see Bierce (2007).

[8] This change established a minimum base amount of $5,000 for the first assessment bracket of the semiannual assessment schedule (total assets up to $2 million). By 2009, the base had increased to $5,580.

[9] These figures reflect annual supervisory assessments and do not include application fees.

[10] National bank figures are computed using the 2007 assessment schedule and assume that banks are in good condition. State assessments are computed using the most recent schedules available on the Web sites of state supervisors.

The last column shows the estimated national bank cost disadvantage for the three asset categories, or the difference between the national bank and state average assessment. The differences shown suggest that supervisory fees are about 50 percent higher for a small national bank than for a similarly sized state bank.

Table 1

Illustrative Estimates of Annual Supervisory Cost Differences in 2007

National Banks vs. Selected State-Chartered Banks

| Asset Size ($ millions) | National Bank | California | Florida | Georgia | Indiana | Louisiana | North Carolina | Texas | State Average | National Bank Disadvantage |
|---|---|---|---|---|---|---|---|---|---|---|
| $25 | $21,000 | $16,300 | $8,000 | $8,000 | $8,700 | $9,600 | $10,000 | $15,500 | $10,871 | $10,129 |
| $50 | $30,000 | $19,700 | $14,000 | $13,800 | $10,500 | $15,500 | $10,000 | $20,300 | $14,829 | $15,171 |
| $100 | $48,200 | $29,400 | $24,500 | $20,900 | $14,800 | $25,000 | $17,000 | $29,400 | $23,000 | $25,200 |

Source: Author's calculations using assessment information from the OCC and state supervisory Web sites.

The magnitude of this cost disadvantage is further highlighted by comparing the supervisory cost differences to total noninterest expenses at relatively small, "young" banks. At year-end 2007, the mean value of noninterest expenses for a national bank less than 10 years old with total assets of $100 million or less was about $499,000 higher than for comparable state banks. The mean total asset size for national and state banks in these two reference groups was about $50 million. The estimated extra supervisory cost burden for a $50 million national bank of $15,171 (see table 1) thus represents about 3.0 percent of its total noninterest cost disadvantage.

In some states, national banks also have lower legal lending limits than state-chartered competitors. As a result, small national banks may be at a disadvantage in lending to commercial borrowers, a profitable group often targeted by de novo banks. The OCC sought to address this potential disadvantage in September 2001 by changing lending limits for small national banks.[11] The changes reduced but did not eliminate the disadvantage for small national banks in all states.

On the other hand, some assert that compliance-related costs may actually be substantially lower for national banks because they need not comply with state laws preempted by the OCC under statutory authority granted by the National Bank Act.[12] This issue has been hotly debated in the wake of the OCC's findings in 2003 and 2004 that federal law preempted the Georgia Fair Lending Act and other state predatory lending laws.[13] Available evidence suggests, however, that larger, geographically diversified national banks are more likely to realize any benefits attributable to preemption.[14] In addition, subsequent revisions in preempted statutes by states and the existence of parity provisions tend to lessen any national bank compliance cost advantages stemming from preemption.

Clearly, nationally chartered de novo banks face a nontrivial supervisory cost disadvantage compared with state banks. But precisely measuring the explicit cost differential (and any implicit cost differential) across states and over time is problematic. The use of time dummies to empirically capture the impact of any charter-related advantages or disadvantages cannot provide clear insight, because the OCC changed its assessment schedule, altered legal

---

[11] In September 2001, the OCC initiated a pilot program permitting eligible national banks to apply for higher lending limits if they were headquartered in states that had higher lending limits for state-chartered banks. In 2004, the program was made permanent. Eligible national banks may apply for higher authority but do not necessarily gain parity with state banks. In addition, de novo banks may not apply for expanded lending authority.

[12] The legal foundation for the OCC's preemption authority is outlined in the *Federal Register* (OCC, 2003, pp. 46120–46123). Recent court cases involving preemption are described in the footnotes. See also Furletti (2004, pp. 3–17), in which the focus is on preemption of state restrictions on credit card issuers. For a less technical discussion, see Texas Finance Commission (2006, pp. 3–8).

[13] In February 2003, the OCC announced that it might preempt the George Fair Lending Act and did so in July 2003. In January 2004, the OCC issued a final preemption rule, outlining the types of state laws that it was likely to preempt in the future.

[14] Whalen (2008).

lending limits for national banks, and preempted state predatory lending laws at roughly the same time.

These measurement issues may help explain why little empirical work has been done to date on the determinants of bank charter choice. The available evidence on charter changes by established banks is consistent with the existence of a competitive disadvantage for those with a national charter. Whalen (2002) examined charter changes by established national banks from 1994 through 2001. That study found a positive, albeit weak, relationship between a national bank's operating expenses and the likelihood that it would switch to a state charter. Whalen also found that national banks more heavily involved in commercial lending—and presumably constrained by tighter lending limits—were more likely to change to state charters. The evidence showed that national banks operating in more competitive local markets were more likely to switch to state charters. This suggests that charter-related disadvantages are more burdensome for banks operating in more competitive markets. Finally, national banks operating in states with larger numbers of previous national-to-state charter conversions also were more likely to switch to state charters. The high number of national banks changing charters could indicate greater actual or perceived benefits to a state charter, more active solicitation of charter flips by state banking regulators, and an increased likelihood that national banks face strong direct competitive pressure from state peers with lower costs.

Recent charter changes by de novo banks provide additional evidence of a competitive disadvantage for small national banks relative to their state-chartered peers. Table 2 shows pure charter flips by six cohorts of de novo banks that began operations with national charters in the six years from 1998 through 2003.[15] The left half of the table shows the number and percentage

---

[15] A pure charter flip is defined as a charter change without a simultaneous change in bank ownership.

8

of de novo banks in each year that started with national charters but switched to state charters by June 30, 2008. The right half shows the number and percentage of de novo banks that began operations with state charters but converted to national banks. The data show that about 10 percent of the de novo banks that opened with national charters during the six-year period switched to state charters. In contrast, only 1 percent of de novo state banks shifted in the opposite direction.

Table 2

Pure Charter Flips by Recent De Novo Banks*

| De Novo Bank Entry Year | Number of De Novo National Banks | Number of De Novo National Banks Flipping to State Charters | Percentage | Number of De Novo State Banks | Number of De Novo State Banks Flipping to National Charters | Percentage |
|---|---|---|---|---|---|---|
| 1998 | 48 | 7 | 14.58 | 114 | 3 | 2.63 |
| 1999 | 55 | 4 | 7.27 | 170 | 1 | 0.59 |
| 2000 | 48 | 4 | 8.33 | 164 | 2 | 1.22 |
| 2001 | 32 | 1 | 3.13 | 105 | 0 | 0.00 |
| 2002 | 32 | 3 | 9.38 | 71 | 0 | 0.00 |
| 2003 | 21 | 4 | 19.05 | 74 | 1 | 1.35 |
| Total | 236 | 23 | 9.75 | 698 | 7 | 1.00 |

*Pure charter flips are defined as charter changes without a simultaneous change in ownership. Data include flips through June 30, 2008.
Source: Author's calculations.

## III. Recent De Novo Bank Entry Patterns

Figure 1 shows a sharp, persistent decline since 2003 in the percentage of de novo banks choosing national charters. An examination of the underlying data illustrates the magnitude of the shift. During the first six years of the sample period (1998–2003), the average value of the annual percentage of de novo banks choosing national charters was 25.5 percent.[16] During the last five years of the sample period (2004–2008), the mean value was 12.9 percent.

---

[16] From 1988 through 1997, the average value was 31 percent.

9

Table 3 shows the number of de novo banks opening in various types of local banking markets from 1998 through 2008. The first row shows the total number and percentage of national- and state-chartered de novo banks that entered the largest urban markets approximated by metropolitan statistical areas. The second row contains similar data for micropolitan areas which are somewhat smaller urban markets. The information for all urban markets in the third row reflects the combined entry numbers for the two types of urban markets presented in the first two rows of the table. The data in the third row also show that about 95 percent of national- and state-chartered de novo banks are concentrated in urban banking markets. The data in the fifth row show that relatively few national and state banks enter non-urban markets. As a result, this study focuses on de novo activity in urban markets.

In table 3, the fourth row shows de novo bank entry in the subset of urban markets that span more than a single state. Somewhat surprisingly, a slightly higher percentage of state de novo banks open for business in interstate urban markets. Assuming de novo banks entering these markets are more likely to branch across state lines, one would expect the opposite to be true if the OCC's preemption authority creates incentives for multistate banks to prefer a national charter.

Table 3

Number and Percentage of De Novo Bank Totals Entering
Alternative Types of Local Markets: 1998-2008

| Type of Market Entered (Total Number of Market Type) | All De Novo Banks | Percent of All De Novo Banks | De Novo National Banks | Percent of All De Novo National Banks | De Novo State Banks | Percent of All De Novo State Banks |
|---|---|---|---|---|---|---|
| Urban Metro Markets (360 Markets) | 1,416 | 85.2 | 278 | 84.5 | 1,138 | 85.3 |
| Urban Micro Markets (569 Markets) | 156 | 9.4 | 37 | 11.3 | 119 | 8.9 |
| All Urban Markets (929 Markets) | 1,572 | 94.5 | 315 | 95.7 | 1,257 | 94.2 |
| Interstate Urban Markets (59 Markets) | 355 | 21.4 | 52 | 15.8 | 303 | 22.7 |
| Nonurban Markets (1319 Markets) | 91 | 5.5 | 14 | 4.3 | 77 | 5.8 |
| Total | 1,663 | | 329 | | 1,334 | |

Source: Author's calculations.

Table 4 shows the scale of national- and state-chartered de novo bank entry across the urban markets in the sample from 1998 through 2008. The first row lists the number of urban markets (out of 929) with at least one de novo bank entrant in a given year. The second row shows the number of urban markets with more than one de novo entrant each year. The numbers in these rows reveal that only a small percentage of urban markets have even a single entrant in a given year and multiple de novo bank entry is even rarer. For example, de novo bank entry occurred in around ten percent of urban markets in 1998, but just 2.7 percent had two or more entrants in that year.

The next four rows of table 4 show the same information for national- and state-chartered entrants separately. Given the small overall number of de novo national banks entrants in a typical year, it is not surprising that the percentage of urban markets with even a single such entrant is very low and hits a maximum of 4.3 percent in 1999. A similar pattern is evident for state banks but both single and multiple entry are more common given the much larger number of such entrants each year.

11

The final row of table 4 shows the number of urban markets gaining both a de novo national- and state-chartered bank in any given year. Comparing these totals to the higher numbers of markets entered by either state or national banks each year indicate that many markets attract entrants with one charter type but not the other. For example, in 1998 only 11 markets had de novo entry by both national and state banks. Since 74 markets had at least one state-chartered entrant, 63 of these markets attracted a new state bank but not a national de novo bank. In addition, the 11 markets gaining both a state- and a national-chartered bank in 1998 represent less than half of the markets (11 out of 25) with multiple entrants. These patterns persist over time, indicating that either the set of factors or the impacts of any common factors affecting de novo bank entry differ across charter types.

Table 4 does not provide any insight on the extent to which the different types of entry are concentrated in the sample markets during the 11-years from 1998 through 2008. The data in table 5 remedy this deficiency. The counts in the table show the number of markets that experienced various types of entry in a given number of years over the period. At one extreme, a given type of entry could have occurred in a specific market in each of the 11 years examined. The number in the bottom left hand corner of the table indicates just six markets had some entry in every year. At the other, a market might experience no entry in every single year over the observations period.

**Table 4**

**Number of Urban Markets Experiencing Different Levels of De Novo Entry by Year: 1998-2008**

| Level of Entry | 1998 | 1999 | 2000 | 2001 | 2002 | 2003 | 2004 | 2005 | 2006 | 2007 | 2008 |
|---|---|---|---|---|---|---|---|---|---|---|---|
| Some De Novo Bank Entry | 97 | 124 | 110 | 88 | 68 | 58 | 61 | 75 | 84 | 82 | 73 |
| More Than One De Novo Bank Entrant | 25 | 38 | 32 | 20 | 16 | 12 | 18 | 25 | 30 | 28 | 21 |
| Some De Novo National Bank Entry | 34 | 40 | 32 | 25 | 25 | 16 | 12 | 18 | 13 | 14 | 13 |
| More Than One De Novo National Bank Entrant | 6 | 8 | 9 | 4 | 6 | 3 | 1 | 2 | 2 | 6 | 2 |
| Some De Novo State Bank Entry | 74 | 100 | 90 | 72 | 47 | 47 | 56 | 68 | 77 | 77 | 67 |
| More Than One De Novo State Bank Entrant | 18 | 26 | 21 | 15 | 12 | 10 | 16 | 20 | 27 | 23 | 19 |
| Both National and State Bank Entry | 11 | 16 | 12 | 9 | 4 | 5 | 7 | 11 | 6 | 9 | 7 |

Source: Author's calculations.

The number in the upper left corner of table 5 shows that 540 markets (58 percent of all urban markets), had no de novo entrants in any of the eleven years examined. An even larger number—783 (or about 84 percent of all urban markets)—gained no new national banks from 1998 through 2008.

Table 5

Number of Years Each Urban Market Had Alternative Types of De Novo Bank Entry: 1998-2008

Type of Entry

| Number of Years with Type of Entry | De Novo Bank Entry | De Novo National Bank Entry | De Novo State Bank Entry | Both De Novo National and State Bank Entry |
|---|---|---|---|---|
| | Number of Urban Markets | Number of Urban Markets | Number of Urban Markets | Number of Urban Markets |
| 0 | 540 | 783 | 589 | 884 |
| 1 | 206 | 103 | 184 | 28 |
| 2 | 75 | 24 | 73 | 6 |
| 3 | 44 | 9 | 34 | 4 |
| 4 | 21 | 2 | 10 | 1 |
| 5 | 6 | 3 | 7 | 2 |
| 6 | 6 | 0 | 7 | 2 |
| 7 | 6 | 2 | 3 | 0 |
| 8 | 5 | 1 | 8 | 0 |
| 9 | 6 | 1 | 3 | 1 |
| 10 | 8 | 1 | 7 | 1 |
| 11 | 6 | 0 | 4 | 0 |
| Total Number of Urban Markets | 929 | 929 | 929 | 929 |

Source: Author's calculations.

Table 6 highlights the potential importance of differences in state supervisory regimes on the charter choices made by de novo banks. The first two columns show the total number of all de novo and national de novo banks in the 10 states with the most entry during the sample period. The totals in the last two rows reveal that this small group of states accounts for 59 percent of all de novos and 66 percent of national de novo banks in the sample. The percent of de novos in each state with national charters during the 11-year period is given in the last column. These percentages vary widely from 50 percent in Texas to 1.6 percent in North Carolina. The wide variation in the national bank de novo percentage suggests that the state-level supervisory or regulatory environment is an important influence on de novo charter choices.

14

Table 6

Charter Preferences in the Ten States with the Most Sample De Novo Banks: 1998-2008

| State | Total Number of De Novo Banks | Total Number of De Novo National Banks | Percentage of State's De Novo Banks with National Charters |
|---|---|---|---|
| Florida | 181 | 28 | 15.5 |
| California | 163 | 36 | 22.1 |
| Georgia | 149 | 36 | 24.2 |
| Texas | 90 | 45 | 50.0 |
| Illinois | 75 | 10 | 13.3 |
| North Carolina | 61 | 1 | 1.6 |
| Tennessee | 58 | 4 | 6.9 |
| Arizona | 56 | 20 | 35.7 |
| Minnesota | 51 | 9 | 17.7 |
| Virginia | 49 | 18 | 36.7 |
| Total Number of De Novo Banks | 933 | 207 | |
| Percent Of Total or National De Novo Banks in the Sample | 59.4 | 65.7 | |

Source: Author's calculations.

## IV. Methodology

The primary aim of this study is to identify the most important factors influencing the charter choices made by de novo banks over time. Annual measures of de novo entry by national and state banks in the 929 urban banking markets in the sample are the basis for the dependent variables used in the estimated equations. Three different econometric models are employed. The distinguishing feature of the three models is the differing definition of the entry measures used as the dependent variables. The following section explains the three models.

### Bivariate Probit Model

The bivariate probit model consists of two related probit equations with correlated disturbances akin to the seemingly unrelated regression model. In this model, the dependent

15

variable in the first equation is set equal to 1 for local markets entered by at least one national de novo bank in year t; otherwise the variable takes a value of 0. The dependent variable in the second equation indicates the presence or absence of local market entry by a de novo state chartered bank in year t. This approach permits the use of different sets of explanatory variables in each related probit equation and allows the effects of any common explanatory variables to vary across the two equations. A disadvantage of this approach is that the binary dependent variables do not reflect differences in entry frequency.

Most of the explanatory variables are the same in the two estimated equations and were chosen from the set of determinants of de novo bank local market entry used in previous empirical research. Several explanatory variables are included only in the de novo national bank entry equation, because they are expected to reflect charter-related advantages or disadvantages faced by national bank entrants. In all the models estimated in the paper, the flow-type explanatory variables are average values calculated over three previous years. The nonflow variables are values measured in year t-4.[17]

Nearly all of the RHS variables common to both equations are measures of local market structure. The first such variable is a Herfindahl-Hirschmann Index of market concentration. Previous studies generally found that concentration has a negative effect on bank entry, ostensibly because it reflects the likelihood of deterrent actions by dominant incumbent organizations in local markets. Some researchers acknowledge the possibility of a positive relationship, reasoning that higher concentration indicates less competition and higher expected profitability for banks in the market.

---

[17] For example, de novo local market entry in 1998 is assumed to depend on merged bank deposits in the market averaged over 1995, 1996, and 1997, and the market concentration level in 1994. The relatively long lag for the static market structure explanatory variables reduces the likelihood that they will be correlated with flow measures of merger activity.

Both estimated equations include two variables that measure the market shares of small and large competitors. Two subjectively chosen cutoffs are used to create the size groups, with $1 billion in organizational deposits as the cutoff for small competitors and $50 billion in deposits for large competitors. These variables are included because evidence suggests that smaller banks are either more willing or better able to satisfy the needs of retail and small commercial customers that value personal service. If this is true, it may be more difficult for new banks to compete for these preferred customer groups in markets where small existing banks are important. The converse also is likely to be true; that is, de novo banks should be able to attract preferred customers more easily in markets where the share of large banks is higher. The expected coefficients on these two variables are negative and positive, respectively.[18]

Existing empirical evidence indicates that de novo bank entry is more likely in markets with more merger and acquisition activity. Studies using more refined merger and acquisition measures found that de novo bank entry is most strongly related to transactions in which targets are small relative to the acquirer and local organizations become part of acquirers headquartered elsewhere. These results are attributed to a short- or long-run unwillingness or inability by larger, nonlocal banks to satisfy small business and retail customers preferring high levels of personal service. The evidence also suggests that mergers of existing affiliates by multibank holding companies (i.e., consolidation mergers) have no impact on de novo entry. Given these results, alternative merger and acquisition definitions incorporating the asset sizes and headquarters of targets and survivors were used in preliminary specifications of the estimated equations. The results led to the use of four merger and acquisition variables in the reported version of the entry

---

[18] Some studies—e.g., Keeton (2000)—include measures of the market share controlled by banking organizations headquartered out-of-market. This type of variable is highly correlated with a measure of the market share controlled by large organizations, so the estimated coefficient of one or the other typically is insignificant in empirical work. This is the reason an out-of-market share variable is not included in any of the estimated equations.

equations.[19] Two of the variables represent holding company acquisition activity in each local market.[20] One represents the percentage of market deposits acquired by holding companies when the transaction creates control by an out-of-state owner; the other the percentage of market deposits acquired in all other types of holding company acquisitions. Two similar variables are used for nonconsolidation merger transactions. The first variable defines the percentage of market deposits merged into a new controlling organization when the transaction also creates control by an out-of-state owner. The second variable defines the percentage of market deposits in all other types of mergers where the targets disappear into a new controlling organization. Given the results reported in previous studies, the anticipated coefficients on the merger and acquisition variables are positive, with those indicating a shift in market share to nonlocal control more likely to be significant.

Both estimated entry equations include a measure of past de novo bank entry, as well as separate variables representing in-market and out-of-market de novo branching. These types of variables have been used in only one of the four previously referenced entry studies. Adams and Amel (2007) define market entry in a given year as the number of de novo banks plus the number of existing organizations that enter the market through out-of-market de novo branches. They find that past entry has a positive influence on current entry and attribute this result to a correlation between past entry and unobserved factors that indicate market attractiveness. They also include a measure of branching by in-market competitors in their equation and expect a

---

[19] Merger and acquisition variables that attempted to capture small-into-large transactions were not more informative than the alternative variables that reflected any shift to out-of-market control.

[20] Holding company formations are excluded.

negative coefficient, because this activity could create a strategic barrier to entry. They find a significant effect only in nonurban markets.

Since past de novo bank and de novo out-of-market branch entry could have different effects on current de novo bank entry, lagged measures of each are used separately in the equations estimated in this study.[21] In both cases, the variables are expressed as entry rates.[22] Similarly, the percentage of existing organizations branching in-market is used as the measure of incumbent branching.

Market size, population, and per capita personal income growth are included in both equations as indicators of the economic attractiveness of local markets. Two market-size dummy variables are used in the equations, because preliminary analysis indicated that the relationship between market size and local market entry is not linear. One variable takes a value of 1 for markets in a given year if the bank deposit total is between the median and 75th percentile value for all urban markets in that year. If not, the value is set equal to 0. The other market size dummy is equal to 1 for markets in the largest deposit quartile in a given year. If expected profitability is higher in larger markets, the estimated coefficients on these variables should be positive.

Two state-level regulatory dummy variables appear in both equations.[23] One indicates whether or not a state had a restriction on intrastate branching in place at the start of the sample period. Although these restrictions were generally eliminated during the period, previous work

---

[21] Adams and Amel (2007) suggest this possibility merits future research.

[22] Entry rates are the number of entrants during a given year divided by the number of banking organizations operating in the market at the start of that year.

[23] Using state-level variables in the analysis is somewhat problematic because of the local market focus and the interstate nature of some urban markets. In this study, each interstate market is assigned to the state that accounts for the highest percentage of total deposits in it.

suggests that the effects of legal barriers to entry persist even after their repeal.[24] The anticipated sign of the coefficient on this variable is positive, because branching restrictions encourage de novo bank entry by reducing competition and the likelihood of preemptive branching by existing organizations.[25] The other state-level regulatory variable in the two entry equations takes a value of 1 for states that permitted interstate branch acquisitions at the start of the period.[26] This variable indicates lower barriers to entry by out-of-state competitors and more intense actual or potential competition, so its coefficient should be negative.

Ten dummy variables representing the years 1999 through 2008 also are included in both equations to control for the effects of macroeconomic forces or any other time-specific influences on the likelihood of local market entry by state and national banks. The expected signs of the year dummies are ambiguous.

Several additional explanatory variables are included only in the entry equation for de novo national banks to reflect any charter-related disadvantages faced by national bank entrants. As previously noted, national banks typically pay higher supervisory costs and have lower legal lending limits than state banks, but the magnitude of these disadvantages varies among states. Since it is problematic to construct good state-specific estimates of any disadvantage over time, three different proxy variables are included to capture the effects of the conjectural competitive disadvantage faced by de novo national banks seeking to enter a given market. The first variable is the ratio of total assets for state-chartered banks headquartered in the state in which the market is located that are not affiliated with multibank holding companies (MBHC) divided by the asset

---

[24] See Stiroh and Strahan (2003).

[25] This variable was constructed using data contained in Conference of State Bank Supervisors (1996, pp. 115–117).

[26] Information in Johnson and Rice (2007, appendix A) was used to construct this variable. Additional state regulatory variables were constructed from the data in this appendix (e.g., a dummy variable reflecting differences in

total for all non-MBHC banks headquartered in the state.[27] Higher values of this ratio presumably reflect a more favorable regulatory environment for state chartered banks and a greater competitive disadvantage for national banks, and so should have a negative effect on national bank de novo local market entry.

The second proxy variable represents the three period average of the net increase in state chartered non-MBHC banks in the state attributable to pure charter flips during a given year divided by the number of state-chartered non-MBHC banks in the state at the beginning of that year. Higher values of this variable indicate more national banks switching to state charters than vice versa and, thus, a greater competitive disadvantage for national banks in that state. Again, the coefficient should be negative in the national bank entry equation.

The third proxy variable is the aggregate local market share of small state-chartered banks. This variable indicates the extent to which any de novo national bank would face direct competition from smaller state chartered institutions in the target market. If state banks have a competitive advantage because of lower supervisory costs or higher legal lending limits, the relationship between this variable and the likelihood of market entry by de novo national banks should be negative.

A dummy variable taking on a value of 1 for local interstate markets and otherwise a value of 0 also is included in the national bank de novo entry equation to reveal any competitive advantage for national banks stemming from the OCC's preemption authority. If de novo banks chartered in interstate markets are more likely to ultimately branch into adjoining states and

---

the minimum acquisition age of banks across states), but the variable described in the text was the only one having a significant effect on de novo bank entry.

[27] Only non-MBHC banks are considered in the calculation of the first two indicators, because local management makes their charter decisions.

preemption reduces expected compliance costs for multistate national banks, the coefficient on this dummy variable should be positive in the national bank de novo entry equation.

The final variable used only in the national bank entry equation is the number of national banks headquartered in the local market that were merged or acquired in a given year divided by the number of banking organizations operating in the market at the start of the year. This variable serves as a measure of the potential supply of experienced key personnel with knowledge of the target market and the OCC. Anecdotal evidence indicates that senior managers of de novo banks typically come from acquisition and merger targets having a similar bank charter.

### *Tobit Model Specifications*

One drawback of the bivariate probit approach is that the dependent variables indicate only the occurrence or nonoccurrence of market entry by national or state banks in a given year. The raw data show that multiple entry by state and national de novo banks occurs in a number of markets each year, but this richer information on entry frequency is not exploited in the bivariate probit model. The data also reveal that a considerable fraction of markets had zero entry by either charter type over the sample period. Tobit models are an econometric alternative that can be used to investigate the determinants of national and state bank local market entry rates when a high percentage of these dependent variables take on zero values.

Two tobit models are used in this study. The first is the bivariate tobit model. Like the bivariate probit model, this model consists of two related charter-specific local market entry equations assumed to have correlated disturbances. But the dependent variables in the two equations in the tobit specification are the de novo national bank and state bank local market entry rates (the number of de novo bank local market entrants of each respective charter type in

22

year t divided by the number of banking organizations in the market in year t-1). The RHS variables in the bivariate tobit versions of the national bank and state bank entry equations are identical to those used in the two equations in the bivariate probit model, with the same anticipated coefficient signs.

Another nonbinary entry variable, providing the clearest insight on de novo bank charter preferences over time, is the percentage of de novo local market entrants in each year that choose a national charter. This entry variable, however, is defined only for the nonrandom sample of local markets in which some entry occurs. This equation can be estimated using a tobit selection model. In this approach, the parameters of a probit selection equation and a tobit equation are estimated jointly using a full information maximum likelihood (FIML) procedure.[28]

The dependent variable in the selection equation has a value of 1 if local market entry by any de novo bank occurs in a given year; otherwise, the value is 0. The set of independent variables used in this equation is the same as that used in the state bank entry equation in the bivariate probit model discussed previously, with the same anticipated signs.

In the related tobit equation, the dependent variable is the number of de novo national bank local market entrants in a given year divided by the number of de novo bank entrants in that year. The independent variables included in the reported version of the tobit equation are a subset of the RHS variables in the national bank de novo market entry equation in the bivariate probit model. The judgmentally determined initial specification of the tobit equation included the set of explanatory variables likely to influence national but not state de novo bank entry, as well as indicators of local market competition, given the expectation that national banks operate at a

---

[28] Because the FIML estimator is used, an additional selection variable is not a RHS variable in the tobit equation, as is the case for two-step limited information estimators of selection models. Insight on the importance of selection in the analysis is provided by the FIML estimate of $\rho$, the correlation between the error terms in the two equations, and its estimated standard error. See Greene (2008), p. E31-3.

relative cost disadvantage. The specification was refined based on the significance of the estimated coefficients in preliminary model runs.

## V. Empirical Results

### *Bivariate Probit Model Results*

Table 7 presents estimates of the two bivariate probit model equations. The coefficients and associated test statistics in the first two columns (Equation 1) reveal the impact of the explanatory variables on the likelihood of national bank local market entry. The next two columns (Equation 2) contain the same information for the determinants of the probability of local market entry by state banks. The estimated value of rho and the associated chi square test statistic—indicating whether or not the error terms in the two equations are significantly correlated—appear in the last rows of the table. The significant test statistic confirms that the two equations should be estimated jointly.

The results for the RHS variables common to both equations are discussed first. The estimation results for the variables appearing only in the national bank entry equation follows.

Higher market concentration significantly reduces the likelihood of both types of entry, and the estimated coefficient in the national bank entry equation is much larger than it is in the equation for state bank entry. The difference in the coefficients across equations is marginally significant. Previous researchers also have found a negative relationship between concentration and the likelihood of de novo bank entry. They argued that this reflects expectations of more intense competitive reactions to entry by incumbent firms that dominate concentrated local markets. If this nontraditional market structure–performance explanation is correct, the estimation results make sense; that is, entry is less likely in more concentrated markets, particularly for national bank entrants with higher costs.

The market share of incumbent small banking organizations has a negative effect on both types of entry, although the effect is highly significant only in the state bank entry equation. The absolute value of the negative coefficient is much larger as well. This finding is at odds with the greater sensitivity of national bank entry to market concentration previously discussed. This result may reflect the effects of multicollinearity, given the additional small state bank market share variable included in the national bank entry equation. The coefficient on the large banking organization market share variable is positive and significant in both equations, and roughly of the same magnitude. This result is consistent with the view that large banking organizations are less willing or able to serve retail and small business customers, creating an opportunity for new banks.

The signs and statistical significance of the four merger and acquisition variables are in line with a priori expectations, with similar results in both equations. All the coefficients are positive and are significant for mergers and acquisitions in which control shifts to an out-of-state owner.

The next three variables in the two equations are measures of different types of lagged entry. Past de novo bank entry is positively related to national and state bank entry but is significant only for the latter. The positive sign suggests that this variable is a proxy for unobserved market-specific factors that stimulate de novo bank entry. Past de novo in-market branching has a similar positive impact on entry by both types of banks, and the estimated coefficients are significant.

The influence of past de novo branching by out-of-market banking organizations on de novo bank entry differs markedly across equations. The estimated coefficient on this variable is negative and is significant only in the national bank market entry equation. This effect could indicate that out-of-market de novo branch entrants tend to be particularly aggressive competitors. They may be more likely to compete on price to build business in a new market, have substantially greater organizational resources than de novo banks, and incur relatively low costs to enter the market through branches. The competitive impact of this type of entry may be particularly important for national de novos with a cost disadvantage.

The market-size dummies indicate that larger urban markets are more likely to experience entry by both types of de novo banks. Market per capita personal income growth and market population growth rates have similar positive, significant effects on national and state bank entry.

In line with expectations, the intrastate branch restriction variable has a positive coefficient in both the national bank and state bank market entry equations. The absence of state restrictions on interstate branch acquisitions has a negative significant impact on both types of entry, presumably because it indicates greater actual or potential competition. Both coefficients are considerably larger in the national bank entry equation, suggesting that national bank entry may be more sensitive to competitive conditions in local markets, consistent with a charter-related cost disadvantage. But the differences in the coefficients across equations are not statistically significant.

The next four explanatory variables reflect the effects of competitive advantages or disadvantages faced by de novo national banks and appear only in the national bank entry equation. The first two variables are proxy measures for the extent of any state-specific competitive disadvantage for national de novo banks relative to state-chartered banks. Higher values of these variables are assumed to reflect a more favorable environment for state chartered banks, all else being equal. The small state-chartered bank market share variable indicates the extent to which a national de novo bank would face competition from similarly sized state banks in its chosen market. In the estimated national bank entry equations, all three variables have the expected negative signs, but only the small state bank market share variable is highly significant. The fourth variable—the interstate market dummy—has a positive coefficient, consistent with a possible national bank preemption advantage, but the variable is not statistically significant.

The last variable, which appears only in the national bank entry equation, represents the extent to which merger and acquisition activity eliminated locally headquartered national banks from the market, presumably creating available senior executive talent familiar to and with the OCC. The estimated coefficient on this variable is positive and significant, consistent with expectations.

Table 7

Bivariate Probit Model For All Urban Markets: 1998-2008[1]

| Dependent Variables | Equation 1 =1 if De Novo National Bank Market Entry Year t | | Equation 2 =1 if De Novo State Bank Market Entry Year t | |
|---|---|---|---|---|
| Independent Variables | COEFF | Z | COEFF | Z |
| Local Market Deposit Concentration (HHI) t-4 | -3.38391 | -4.90*** | -1.77355 | -4.25*** |
| Deposit Market Share of Banking Organizations w/ Assets < $1 billion t-4 | -0.25685 | -1.25 | -0.81088 | -5.83*** |
| Deposit Market Share of Banking Organizations w/ Assets > $50 billion t-4 | 0.82656 | 3.96 | 0.61806 | 4.31*** |
| Avg. % of Market Deposits Acquired: Deal Creates Out-of-State Holding Company Owner | 3.47702 | 3.57*** | 2.53259 | 3.56*** |
| Avg. % of Market Deposits Acquired: All Other Holding Company Acquisitions | 0.89894 | 0.98 | 0.16223 | 0.23 |
| Avg. % of Market Deposits Acquired: Nonconsolidation Mergers, Deal Creates New Out-of-State Holding Company Owner | 1.79269 | 1.47 | 3.19432 | 4.16*** |
| Avg. % of Market Deposits Acquired: All Other Nonconsolidation Mergers | 1.26951 | 1.39 | 0.22018 | 0.30 |
| Avg. Market De Novo Bank Entry Rate | 1.51086 | 0.87 | 2.46390 | 1.99** |
| Avg. Market De Novo In-Market Branch Rate | 1.34082 | 3.08*** | 1.81939 | 5.06*** |
| Avg. Market De Novo Out-of-Market Branch Rate | -2.57850 | -2.19** | -0.16167 | -0.23 |
| Market Deposit Size Dummy: 50-75th Percentile t-4 | 0.06064 | 0.60 | 0.26272 | 3.65*** |
| Market Deposit Size Dummy: Top Quartile t-4 | 0.34165 | 3.18*** | 0.80623 | 9.97*** |
| Avg. Market Per Capita Annual Personal Income Growth | 0.04131 | 1.91* | 0.05361 | 3.75*** |
| Avg. Market Annual Population Growth | 0.08487 | 2.79*** | 0.10601 | 4.56*** |
| Intrastate Branching Limited in State 1997 | 0.30591 | 2.59*** | 0.18562 | 2.39** |
| Interstate Branch Acquisition Permitted in State 1997 | -0.30011 | -2.90*** | -0.17825 | -2.74*** |
| Asset of non-MBHC State Chartered Banks Headquartered in State/Assets All non-MBHC Banks Headquartered in State t-4 | -0.39668 | -1.69* | | |
| Avg. Net Increase in State Chartered non-MBHC Banks from Pure Charter Flips in State/Number of State Chartered non-MBHC Banks in State | -15.48550 | -1.91* | | |
| Deposit Market Share of State Chartered Banks w/ Assets < $1 bilion t-4 | -0.73043 | -3.10*** | | |
| Interstate Market Dummy | 0.17454 | 1.45 | | |
| Avg. Number of National Banks Headquartered in Market Merged or Acquired/ Number of Banking Organizations in Market | 3.40075 | 3.31*** | | |
| Constant | -1.50363 | -5.51*** | -1.82843 | -9.48*** |
| Number of Observations | 10219 | | | |
| chi2 | 918.1*** | | | |
| rho | 0.1942 | | | |
| Wald test rho=0 chi2(1) | 10.61*** | | | |

[1]Annual time dummies were also included in these equations but are not reported in the table.
***,**,* Significant at the 1, 5, and 10 percent level, respectively.

Source: Author's calculations.

## Bivariate Tobit Model Results

Table 8 shows the estimation results for the bivariate tobit model. The specification of each entry equation is the same as the one used in the bivariate probit model, but the dependent variables are national and state bank local market entry rates, respectively, rather than simple binary market entry variables. As in table 7, the dependent variable in Equation 1 is the national bank entry rate. The dependent variable in Equation 2 is the state bank entry rate.

Comparison of the results in tables 7 and 8 reveals that changing the definition of the dependent variables and the econometric model produces very few differences in the sign and significance of the estimates. Again, the results indicate that the national bank de novo entry rate is somewhat more sensitive than the state bank entry rate to market competition indicators. In particular, market concentration and out-of-market de novo branching appear to have much stronger impacts on national bank de novo entry than on state bank entry.

Several differences are evident in the estimated effects of the RHS variables that appear only in the national bank entry rate equation compared with the bivariate probit version. In the bivariate tobit model, the estimated coefficient on the share of state-level non-MBHC institution assets controlled by state banks is again negative, but its statistical significance is considerably reduced. Conversely, the coefficient on the percentage increase in state-chartered banks attributable to charter flips remains negative as in the bivariate probit case, but it is statistically significant in the bivariate tobit specification.

Table 8

Bivariate Tobit Model For All Urban Markets: 1998-2008[1]

| Dependent Variables | Equation 1 | | Equation 2 | |
|---|---|---|---|---|
| | De Novo National Bank Entrants Year t/ Number of Banking Organizations Year t-1 | | De Novo State Bank Entrants Year t/ Number of Banking Organizations Year t-1 | |
| Independent Variables | COEFF | Z | COEFF | Z |
| Local Market Deposit Concentration (HHI) t-4 | -0.41357 | -2.46** | -0.17030 | -3.85*** |
| Deposit Market Share of Banking Organizations w/ Assets < $1 billion t-4 | -0.03509 | -0.86 | -0.10204 | -5.76*** |
| Deposit Market Share of Banking Organizations w/ Assets > $50 billion t-4 | 0.11742 | 2.72*** | 0.07450 | 4.32*** |
| Avg. % of Market Deposits Acquired: Deal Creates Out-of-State Holding Company Owner | 0.51633 | 3.05*** | 0.39008 | 4.57*** |
| Avg. % of Market Deposits Acquired: All Other Holding Company Acquisitions | 0.09822 | 0.65 | 0.04243 | 0.51 |
| Avg. % of Market Deposits Acquired: Nonconsolidation Mergers, Deal Creates New Out-of-State Holding Company Owner | 0.27876 | 1.33 | 0.45409 | 4.20*** |
| Avg. % of Market Deposits Acquired: All Other Nonconsolidation Mergers | 0.24138 | 1.30 | 0.07121 | 0.80 |
| Avg. Market De Novo Bank Entry Rate | 0.00147 | 0.50 | 0.00132 | 0.75 |
| Avg. Market De Novo In-Market Branch Rate | 0.19581 | 1.96** | 0.18625 | 3.71*** |
| Avg. Market De Novo Out-of-Market Branch Rate | -0.36099 | -2.21** | 0.02605 | 0.32 |
| Market Deposit Size Dummy: 50-75th Percentile t-4 | 0.00926 | 0.43 | 0.03886 | 4.08*** |
| Market Deposit Size Dummy: Top Quartile t-4 | 0.04879 | 1.76* | 0.10290 | 7.36*** |
| Avg. Market Per Capita Annual Personal Income Growth | 0.59567 | 1.40 | 0.67263 | 3.07*** |
| Avg. Market Annual Population Growth | 0.01322 | 2.33** | 0.01584 | 5.57*** |
| Intrastate Branch Limited in State 1997 | 0.04667 | 2.34** | 0.02941 | 3.29 |
| Interstate Branch Acquisition Permitted in State 1997 | -0.04665 | -2.67*** | -0.01898 | -2.52** |
| Asset of non-MBHC State Chartered Banks Headquartered in State/Assets All non-MBHC Banks Headquartered in State t-4 | -0.05373 | -1.03 | | |
| Avg. Net Increase in State Chartered non-MBHC Banks from Pure Charter Flips in State/Number of State Chartered non-MBHC Banks in State | -0.02531 | -2.58*** | | |
| Deposit Market Share of State Chartered Banks w/ Assets < $1 billion t-4 | -0.10551 | -2.26** | | |
| Interstate Market Dummy | 0.02594 | 1.27 | | |
| Avg. Number of National Banks Headquartered in Market Merged or Acquired/ Number of Banking Organizations in Market | 0.50329 | 2.62*** | | |
| Constant | -0.26284 | -5.32*** | -0.26227 | -10.37*** |
| Number of Observations | 10219 | | | |
| sigma(1) | 0.16222 (8.31***) | | | |
| sigma(2) | .14131 (20.12***) | | | |
| rho (1,2) | .13701 (2.33**) | | | |

[1]Annual time dummies were also included in these equations but are not reported in the table.
***,**,* Significant at the 1, 5, and 10 percent level, respectively.

Source: Author's calculations.

## Tobit Selection Model Results

The estimation results for this model are in table 9. The first two columns contain the estimates of the probit selection equation, which has a binary market de novo bank entry indicator as the dependent variable. Since most of the observed market entry over the period reflects the action of state banks, it is not surprising that the signs and statistical significance of the estimated coefficients on the RHS variables in the probit selection equation are basically the same as the bivariate probit estimates of the state bank market entry equation (Equation 2) in table 7. The coefficient estimates of the RHS variables in the selection equation are, however, of secondary interest in this model and so are not discussed in detail. The probit equation is important in the analysis primarily because incorporating selection effects in the model produces corrected coefficient estimates and associated test statistics for the explanatory variables in the associated tobit national bank entry share equation.

The selection-adjusted estimates of the tobit equation (which has the percentage of all local market de novo bank entrants with national charters as the dependent variable) appear in last two columns of table 9. In most cases, the signs and significance of the estimated coefficients on the included RHS variables are similar to those observed in the bivariate probit and tobit versions of the national bank entry equations.

The results show that the percentage of de novo entrants with national charters is significantly influenced by market concentration. The negative coefficient on the Herfindahl-Hirschmann Index means that this measure of national bank entry is lower in markets with higher market concentration, all else being equal. A plausible explanation for this relationship is that predatory behavior by dominant incumbent firms is more likely in concentrated markets, discouraging de novo entry by cost-disadvantaged national banks.

The estimated coefficient on the out-of-market branching variable also is negative and significant in the tobit equation in the selection model. Competition is greater in local markets with more de novo branch entry by out-of-market firms, reducing the percentage of higher cost de novo bank entrants with national charters.

The explanatory variables in the tobit equation that exhibit signs substantially different from those in the other models are the market-size dummies. In the tobit equation, the estimated coefficients on the two variables are negative and, for the largest market class, significant. These results suggest that the national bank percentage of total de novo bank entrants is lower in larger markets. One possible explanation for this finding is the following. While larger markets might be more economically attractive and encouraging to entrants, actual and potential competition especially from nonbank firms also may be higher in these markets. If market size does incorporate the effects of unobserved potential competition, and cost-disadvantaged national bank de novo entrants are more sensitive to this, the national bank portion of market entrants would tend to be lower in larger markets.

The intrastate branching restriction dummy has the expected positive sign, although the significance level is marginal. The coefficient on the dummy variable indicating the absence of restrictions on interstate branch acquisitions has the anticipated negative sign and is weakly significant. These results indicate that lower barriers to branch expansion increase market competition and discourage entry by national banks with higher costs.

The three variables intended to capture the extent of any state-specific competitive disadvantage for national banks all have negative coefficients—as they did in the bivariate probit and tobit models—and all are statistically significant. The fraction of de novo entrants with national charters is lower in local markets in states where state banks have a larger asset share and where charter flips produced a larger increase in state bank charters. The percentage of de novo national bank entry also is lower in local markets where entrants face greater direct competition from small state-chartered banks (reflected in a larger aggregate market share).

As in the other econometric models, the coefficient on the dummy interstate market variable is insignificant. This result does not support the notion that the OCC's preemption authority creates significant benefits for small national banks.

The coefficient on the measure of recent mergers and acquisitions of locally headquartered national banks is positive and significant in the estimated tobit equation. This result is consistent with the view that the merger variable represents the potential supply of available, experienced senior managers who know the target market and are familiar with and to national bank supervisors. Thus, the percentage of new banks with national charters tends to be higher in local markets where the potential management supply is more abundant.

Table 9

Tobit Selection Model For All Urban Markets: 1998-2008[1]

| Dependent Variables | Probit Selection Equation | | Tobit Equation | |
|---|---|---|---|---|
| | =1 if De Novo Bank Market Entry in Year t | | De Novo National Bank Entrants in Market in Year t/ Total Number of De Novo Entrants in Market in Year t | |
| Independent Variables | COEFF | Z | COEFF | Z |
| Local Market Deposit Concentration (HHI) t-4 | -1.92305 | -9.05*** | -1.77776 | -2.06** |
| Deposit Market Share of Banking Organizations w/ Assets < $1 billion t-4 | -0.71335 | -7.48*** | | |
| Deposit Market Share of Banking Organizations w/ Assets > $50 billion t-4 | 0.71796 | 7.49*** | | |
| Avg. % of Market Deposits Acquired: Deal Creates Out-of-State Holding Company Owner | 3.08949 | 6.40*** | | |
| Avg. % of Market Deposits Acquired: All Other Holding Company Acquisitions | 0.46523 | 0.96 | | |
| Avg. % of Market Deposits Acquired: Nonconsolidation Mergers, Deal Creates New Out-of-State Holding Company Owner | 2.83378 | 4.37*** | | |
| Avg. % of Market Deposits Acquired: All Other Nonconsolidation Mergers | 0.63047 | 1.19 | | |
| Avg. Market De Novo Bank Entry Rate | 0.02356 | 2.48** | | |
| Avg. Market De Novo In-Market Branch Rate | 1.83384 | 7.21*** | | |
| Avg. Market De Novo Out-of-Market Branch Rate | -0.45680 | -0.95 | -3.04314 | -2.07** |
| Market Deposit Size Dummy: 50-75th Percentile t-4 | 0.25180 | 4.99*** | -0.35229 | -1.62 |
| Market Deposit Size Dummy: Top Quartile t-4 | 0.79879 | 14.07*** | -0.58874 | -2.16** |
| Avg. Market Per Capita Annual Personal Income Growth | 5.46734 | 4.71*** | | |
| Avg. Market Annual Population Growth | 0.10548 | 6.84*** | | |
| Intrastate Branch Limit in State 1997 | 0.22585 | 4.56*** | 0.22279 | 1.70* |
| Interstate Branch Acquisition Permitted in State 1997 | -0.20575 | -4.89*** | -0.24948 | -1.89* |
| Asset of non-MBHC State Chartered Banks Headquartered in State/Assets All non-MBHC Banks Headquartered in State t-4 | | | -1.12904 | -2.74*** |
| Avg. Net Increase in State Chartered non-MBHC Banks from Pure Charter Flips in State/Number of State Chartered non-MBHC Banks in State | | | -0.22495 | -2.61*** |
| Deposit Market Share of State Chartered Banks w/ Assets < $1 bilion t-4 | | | -0.69559 | -1.96** |
| Interstate Market Dummy | | | -0.06301 | -0.48 |
| Avg. Number of National Banks Headquartered in Market Merged or Acquired/ Number of Banking Organizations in Market | | | 3.33598 | 2.88*** |
| Constant | -1.64929 | -14.54*** | 0.93458 | 1.91* |
| Number of Observations | 10219 | | | |
| sigma (1) | 1.04763 (7.31***) | | | |
| rho (1,2) | -.15841 (-1.39) | | | |

[1]Annual time dummies were also included in these equations but are not reported in the table.

***,**,* Significant at the 1, 5, and 10 percent level, respectively.

Source: Author's calculations.

## VI. Summary and Conclusions

Examination of the charter choices made by the 1,663 new banks established from 1998 through 2008 reveals that since 2003 there has been a marked, persistent shift in preferences away from the national charter. To explain this change in trend, we investigated the determinants of the charter choices of de novo banks entering urban banking markets during this 11-year period.

Three different econometric models, using alternative annual measures of national bank and state bank local market entry, helped determine whether or not the results are robust.

In two models—the bivariate probit and the bivariate tobit models—separate equations for national bank and state bank de novo local market entry with differing specifications are estimated jointly. While the dependent market entry variables differ slightly in these two models the coefficient estimates in both cases are basically the same. Explanatory variables common to the paired entry equations generally had similar effects on both national and state bank local market entry. There are, however, several exceptions. State intrastate branching restrictions had a significant positive effect only on the likelihood of national bank local market entry. While higher market concentration has a significant negative impact on the probability of both types of entry, the effect was considerably larger for national bank entry. Another variable having a materially different effect on national and state bank entry is the measure of de novo branching by out-of-market banking organizations. The estimated coefficient on this variable is negative and significant only in the national bank entry equation. Taken together, these three results suggest that higher supervisory costs may make national bank entry more sensitive to local market competitive conditions.

The variables included only in the national bank local market entry equation generally exhibit the anticipated signs, although only one was highly significant. National bank entry was less likely to occur in markets located in states where state chartered banks have a larger aggregate deposit share and more banks have switched from a national to a state charter. Entry also was less likely the greater the local market share of small, state chartered banks. These variables seem to reflect the importance of state-specific supervisory disadvantages and the extent to which new national banks would have to compete directly against banks with state charters. The variable measuring the disappearance of locally headquartered national banks through merger and acquisition activity did have a significant positive effect on national bank local market entry. This link likely reflects the availability of senior management familiar with and to national bank supervisors. The results do not show that national bank entry is significantly more likely in interstate markets, suggesting that entrants expect minimal preemption benefits.

The third model was a tobit selection model. The dependent variable in the tobit equation in this model is the percentage of de novo bank local market entrants with a national charter in each year. The probit selection equation adjusts the tobit estimates to reflect the fact that the dependent variable is observed only in markets in which some entry occurs.

The estimated impacts of the explanatory variables in the tobit equation generally are consistent with those in the bivariate probit and bivariate tobit models. Higher values of state-level state bank asset share, national-to-state bank charter flips, and small state bank local market share are associated with lower percentages of national bank de novo entrants. Greater numbers of mergers and acquisitions of locally headquartered national banks had a significant positive effect on the national bank de novo entry percentage.

The two other variables with the strongest direct impacts on the national de novo entry percentage were market concentration and out-of-market de novo branch entry. Both coefficients were negative and significant. These results are consistent with a charter-related cost disadvantage for de novo national banks.

A number of interesting questions and extensions warrant further examination. Better estimates of state-specific charter-related disadvantages could be developed. It also may be possible to develop rough estimates of differences in implicit supervisory costs for de novo banks using data on enforcement actions or other supervisory information. De novo charter choice could be explored using bank-level information for new entrants, which for example, might reveal the impact of a bank's initial strategy. Finally, de novo bank entrants could be followed over time to determine if they perform in ways consistent with the evidence reported in this study. If de novo national banks do face an initial cost disadvantage, they should underperform their state-chartered peers or possibly be more likely to flip their charters.

## References

Adams, R., and D. Amel. 2007. *The Effects of Past Entry, Market Consolidation, and Expansion by Incumbents on the Probability of Entry*. Working Paper 2007-51. Board of Governors of the Federal Reserve System Finance and Economics Discussion Series.

Berger, A., S. Bonime, L. Goldberg, and L. White. 2000. The Dynamics of Market Entry: The Effects of Mergers and Acquisitions on Entry in the Banking Industry. *Proceedings From a Conference on Bank Structure and Competition*, Federal Reserve Bank of Chicago.

Bierce, M. 2007. Charter Smarter. *SNL De Novo Digest*, (April 17, 2007).

Blair, C., and R. Kushmeider. 2006. Challenges to the Dual Banking System: The Funding of Bank Supervision. *FDIC Banking Review*, 18, 1–20.

Conference of State Bank Supervisors. 1996. *A Profile of State Chartered Banking*. Washington, D.C.

Furletti, M. 2004. *The Debate Over the National Bank Act and the Preemption of State Efforts to Regulate Credit Cards*. Discussion Paper 04-02. Payment Cards Center, Federal Reserve Bank of Philadelphia.

Greene, W. 2008. LIMDEP Version 9.0 Econometric Modeling Guide, Vol. 2., Econometric Software, Inc., Plainview, NY.

Johnson, C., and T. Rice. 2007. *Assessing a Decade of Interstate Bank Branching*. Working Paper 2007-03. Federal Reserve Bank of Chicago.

Keeton, W. 2000. Are Mergers Responsible for the Surge in New Charters? *Federal Reserve Bank of Kansas City Economic Review,* (First Quarter), 21–41.

Office of the Comptroller of the Currency. 2003. Notice: Preemption Determination and Order. *Federal Register*, 68, 46264–46281.

Rosen, R. 2003. Is Three a Crowd? Competition Among Regulators in Banking. *Journal of Money, Credit and Banking*, 35(6, part 1), 967–998.

Seelig, S., and T. Critchfield. 2003. *Merger Activity as a Determinant of De Novo Entry into Urban Banking Markets*. FDIC Working Paper 2003-01.

Stiroh, K., and P. Strahan. 2003. Competitive Dynamics of Deregulation: Evidence From U.S. Banking. *Journal of Money, Credit and Banking*, 35(5), 801–828.

Texas Finance Commission. 2006. *Preemption of Financial Services Study*. December.

Whalen, G. 2002. *Charter Flips by National Banks*. Working Paper 2002-1. Washington,DC: Office of the Comptroller of the Currency.

Whalen, G. 2008. The Impact of the Preemption of the Georgia Fair Lending Act by the OCC on National and State Banks and the Dual Banking System. *Quarterly Review of Economics and Finance*, 48, 772–791.

www.ingramcontent.com/pod-product-compliance
Lightning Source LLC
Chambersburg PA
CBHW052021280526
45793CB00005B/1075